How to Pay Off Credit Card Debt

by Sue Maddock

Text copyright © 2012 S L Maddock

All Rights Reserved

Table of Contents

Pick a Card, ANY Card. 6

Pick a Number, but NOT just any Number. 8

Make it Happen, Make it Habit. 10

Congratulations, you've made it Happen. 11

Make It Habit 11

Your Mindset 14

The Avalanche Starts 15

How Does It Work? 16

The Avalanche 19

What Happens When I've Paid Off My Card? 22

What Not To Do 27

What Happens in an Emergency? 31

Need more help, or willing to share your story? 34

Congratulations!

By purchasing this guide you have proved you have the

DESIRE

and the

CAPABILITY

to pay off your credit card debt.

Well Done!

So let's get started ...

Pick a Card, ANY Card.

If, like me, you have multiple credit cards, then you need to know where to start - which credit card do you start paying off first? If you are really like me then your problem is actually getting started, doing something that will make a difference! A long winded explanation of how to choose which credit card to start with does not help. So we are not going to worry about it. The best thing for this system is to start with the card with the lowest balance on it, but if you don't want to do it that way (or don't even want to look at the balances!) then pick any card and stop worrying about whether it is the right choice or not.

An important thing with this system is for you to continue paying off your credit cards the same way as you have been doing up to now - if you generally pay off the minimum amount each month, like I used to do, then continue doing that with all your cards (your chosen one included) whilst you follow this system.

If you are in the unfortunate situation where you are not even managing to pay off the minimum amount each month then the best thing would be to talk to the credit card companies - they may even be able to stop the interest accruing - and propose a minimum amount you will pay each month (we'll discuss how much that is shortly), then follow this system but split the money between all of your cards. NOTE: unless you are in this situation DO NOT split the payments from this system across multiple cards, just stick to paying your normal amount off all cards other than the chosen one.

So stop worrying, don't fret about it, and make the simplest decision you are comfortable with. Go on, do it NOW, pick a credit card, ANY card.

My Card is

_____

Pick a Number, but NOT just any Number.

When you purchased this guide you paid the equivalent of $5, and you said you could afford to pay that amount and it would not have a severe affect on your day. It's funny how we can spend $5 and not really miss it. Since I know you can spend $5 and not severely miss it, that is the minimum number you are going to pick. (Note: If this is not your currency then just use a nice rounded number in your own currency that is close to this amount.)

If you could have spent more on this guide and not really missed it; still considered it an "impulse buy"; then increase your number. Be honest with this, it is amazing how much we can just "waste" in a day and it has little or no affect on us - do you miss the money for that coffee at lunch time? Do you miss the money for the newspaper each morning? Do you miss the money for your lottery ticket? I am not saying you need to stop these things, far from it. What I am saying is there is an amount which you can spend without really noticing it - you proved that by just paying $5 to read this! So if you think you could have spent $10 on this guide and not really missed it (note the "could have", not "would have" - I am not asking you to judge the value of this guide, just how much money you "could have" afforded to pay had you wanted to), but had you spent $11 then you would have to think harder about it; then your number is $10. If you feel you could have spent $20 on this guide, but if you spent

$21 you would be feeling the pinch; then your number is $20. Some of you may feel you could have spent $100 on this guide had you wanted to, and not been too affected for the day, but if you spent $110 then it would no longer have been that "impulse" purchase; then your number is $100.

Personally, when I started this system my number was £10 (I'm in the UK so my currency is £) - if I thought about the "big" picture this number seemed too high for me, that's why I want you to choose your number BEFORE you see the "big" picture, just think about TODAY. Be brave, don't think too much about it, you will be surprised what a difference even $5 will make and how little you will miss it, but if you can make it a bit more then please do.

When I first started this system my debts amounted to around £50,000 - not that I ever wanted to face adding them up! So if you think the number you have seems very small compared to the size of your debt, stop worrying, mine was less than a peanut compared to the overall debt.

So go on, pick a number (but NOT just any number), how much could you have paid for this guide without really worrying about the cost?

My Number is

_____

Make it Happen, Make it Habit.

You've now done all the hard thinking, now you just have to take the action and make it HABIT.

Take YOUR NUMBER and pay it off YOUR CARD - do it NOW, you're not going to miss it, you've already told me that. Don't worry about the fact that you feel it will not make any difference to that big balance (remember my balance was around £50,000 and my number was just £10), just do it, DO IT NOW.

If you use internet banking then this step is easy, just log into your account and set up a payment for YOUR NUMBER to YOUR CARD, don't worry that it seems a petty amount to pay, these systems are automated, nobody is judging you. Stop thinking about it, DO IT NOW.

If you do not have access to internet banking and have to pay your credit card at the bank, don't panic, and no, you're not going to escape. Take YOUR NUMBER and put it into a piggy bank, a tin or any secure place where it can be stored - DO IT NOW - you can take it to the bank and pay it off YOUR CARD when it is convenient.

Have you done that? Is YOUR NUMBER now paid off YOUR CARD or stored in a safe place ready to be paid off? If YES then

Congratulations, you've made it Happen.

That's it, that's all you need to do today - well, almost. Was it painful? Are you really going to miss this money today? Be proud of yourself, you have taken your first step to paying off those headache creating credit cards.

Okay, before you put the kettle on, of grab a beer from the fridge, there is just one more thing you need to do today, then you can spend the rest of the day without thinking about those awful debts. What you NEED to do is put a reminder in your diary, on your telephone or anywhere you will be certain to see it, to do the same again tomorrow - pay off YOUR NUMBER from YOUR CARD. Go on, before you sit down and relax, take the first step to ...

Make It Habit

Don't underestimate this step, it's crucial that you set that reminder, you are going to make this a habit, set a reminder **EVERY DAY**.

When I first started this system I would write the name of the card I was focussing on the next day in my diary to remind me to make the payment. As time went on and I started to feel really good about my debts I began also putting the balance of the card down; and each day I would reduce it by the amount I had just paid off - it does help. However, you may not be ready to face the balances yet (I wasn't at first) so don't fret about it, just set the reminder to make that payment - you wont miss the money, so DO IT - no pain.

If this is all you want to read that's fine. There are no other compulsory actions you need to take; although you will no doubt find yourself taking all the actions I discuss later without me ever telling you to - that's where the BIG GAINS come. If you want to know in advance how this will avalanche into you paying off your credit card debt quicker than you could have imagined then by all means, read on. If not, then the only other reading I would recommend is the section on What Not to Do.

A couple of side notes before I continue. If you are collecting your money in a safe place try to get to the bank and pay it off your credit card each week rather than waiting until the end of the month.

The second side note for those people who are not managing to pay off their minimum balances at the moment. If this is you then try alternating your credit cards each day so, say you have four cards, pay YOUR NUMBER off Card 1 on Day 1, YOUR NUMBER off Card 2 on Day 2, YOUR NUMBER off Card 3 on Day 3, YOUR NUMBER off Card 4 on Day 4, then back to YOUR NUMBER off Card 1 on Day 5. Once you have reached the minimum payment on a card drop it from the list unless it was chosen as YOUR CARD in the first section, in which case keep it on the list so you end up paying above the minimum. Hopefully by the end of the month you will only be paying off YOUR

CARD, as you will have managed to pay the minimum off the others. If doing this still does not cover the minimum balances on all of your credit cards then you really need to be speaking with your credit card suppliers and taking some action to consolidate your debts.

Your Mindset

This system is not based on a mathematical calculation that proves how paying $5 off your credit card debt every day can rid you of debt fast and permanently - and that's surprising since I'm a mathematician! This system is based on getting you in the right mindset to enable you to make the BIG GAINS with NO PAIN.

If you are anything like me, and I don't think I'm that unusual (although some would disagree!), then when your debt has become out of hand the last thing you want to do is face it. It's depressing! The only thing you monitor is if there is enough space left on the card to buy that new dress you fancy, to go out to dinner, or just to buy a bottle of gin to drown your sorrows with.

When people start talking about credit card debt all you hear is the massive call for you to face everything you have been burying your head in the sand to avoid. What are you told? *"Calculate exactly how much you owe"* , *"Compare the interest rates for every debt"*; *"Develop a detailed monthly budget for your spending"* ... Then ... *"cut up your credit cards."*; *"Freeze them in ice"* ... Still Struggling? ... *"Get a part time job to earn more money"*; *"Stop going out"*; *"Sell your body parts to medical science"* ... And what do you do? Bury your head further in the sand of course!

This system is designed so that you do not have to bring your head out of the sand until YOU are ready. No calculation of how much you owe. No determining which credit card is charging you the highest interest rate. No setting budgets - which you are only going to break anyway. No cutting your cards up, or even your spending down. You even get to keep all your body parts and your spare time. In fact, NO PAIN.

You can happily keep your head in the sand, just do the two minute actions each day:

Pay off YOUR NUMBER from YOUR CARD

Set a REMINDER to do the same again tomorrow

That's all you need to do to get started. Once you have done this for a while your head will naturally come out of the sand. When this happens things get really interesting ...

The Avalanche Starts

How Does It Work?

But before we talk about the Avalanche, let's just explain a little of how this very simple system works for you in big ways.

One thing you need to be aware of is this system does not do any fancy footwork to magically make a large (or even small) portion of your debts disappear. With this system you will be paying off your debts legitimately, right down to the last cent. Sorry to be harsh, but you created the debts, you enjoyed the fruits of the purchases you made, so you have to pay them off. If you are looking for an "Abracadabra" plan to make your debts magically disappear then I'm afraid you are in the wrong place. Here we are going to take responsibility for our actions and we are going to get a grip on it.

What this system does is it reduces, and ultimately eliminates, your debts. You may be thinking "how, in my lifetime, will I ever eliminate my debts by just paying $5 per day off them?" Just remember, great trees come from small seeds, and once that seed gets hold then there is no stopping it.

The biggest barrier to us achieving anything is our own minds. Whilst all we are doing is worrying about the immensity of our debt, and that it is just too big to be able to handle, then we tend to do very little other than buy headache tablets in the hope that it will alleviate the stress -

believe me, it won't. In order to get you to face your debts and do what is required to get them under control we need to change your mindset. We need to stop thinking negatively about the debts and start thinking in a positive way. Only when we start thinking positively can we really make inroads into dealing with the debts and start living a happy, headache free life again.

What this system will do, if you follow it, is change your mindset. It will turn your negative feelings into positive ones - you don't need to work on that, the system will make it happen naturally. And once you have positive feelings towards your debts then amazing things can happen. Just $5 per day being paid off one of your credit cards can create unbelievable momentum on the journey to becoming debt free - trust me, I've been there.

Remember, you are not asking yourself to make any real sacrifices, just an amount you can comfortably do without on a daily basis. You are not trying to change your spending behaviour. You are not trying to work harder or play less. Just do the two steps:

Pay off YOUR NUMBER from YOUR CARD

Set a REMINDER to do the same again tomorrow

and after a week or two just watch your attitude towards your debts change completely.

One VERY IMPORTANT point, DO NOT change the system to paying off an amount on a weekly basis rather than daily. The daily aspect is VERY important in changing your mindset. If it is difficult for you to make payments on one particular day in the week - I found weekends when I was not in the office difficult - then skip that day. But make sure you pay YOUR NUMBER from YOUR CARD religiously on all the other days.

The absolute key to this system working is that you create a daily habit in making a difference, no matter how small, to your debt. Do that and your mindset will change to help you.

The Avalanche

So now you want to know how such a little trickle can cause a massive avalanche? What I describe here is very likely to happen to you whether you read this section or not. However, don't think that you HAVE TO take any of these steps. These are some of the things I have experienced due to my change in mindset created from paying off MY NUMBER from MY CARD, DAILY. If you do that, your mindset will change too, and every other action becomes natural.

For this section please remember, these things happen once you are in a positive mindset towards your debts. If you are still in the negative mindset then please do not get stressed out by the thought of having to achieve these things - YOU DON'T, it will happen naturally.

After paying off my amount from my first card for a while, I started checking the balance (my head was totally buried in the sand before this!) I even started writing the balance beside my daily reminder, and reducing it by my £10 each day once I had paid it off. Then, when I saw it getting close to a milestone - for me this was a multiple of £1,000 - I became very keen to get it below the milestone. I would check my bank balance and wonder if I could afford to pay a bit extra just to push it down, and it was amazing how often I could. So one day, when there was a bit of spare money, I would pay off a lump sum to push it under the milestone - I felt GREAT! Then I would go back to my £10 a day and continue to the next milestone.

Did paying this extra lump sum affect my life? Maybe. If I hadn't paid it off my credit card I would have spent it on something else, probably wasted it. I never put us in financial difficulty, but I did make us less well off than we could have been. But it didn't matter, I felt great, REALLY GREAT! The positivity that came to me from passing a milestone was worth a little sacrifice, definitely. But remember, you don't need to make any sacrifice, not unless you get to the point I did, and you want to. When you want to do it, and it makes you feel so good, well, it's no longer a sacrifice. So, with these added little boosts, my debt was reducing even faster.

Then came the time when I was close to paying off my first card - WOW, was I excited. In fact, I was far too excited to wait! As soon as I could get my hands on enough money to finish it off, that's exactly what I did. Did I consider it a sacrifice? Not at all, I was jubilant! I couldn't have been happier. For the first time in years I had a credit card which had NOTHING on it. Yippee!!!

Had I taken the time to calculate how long it would take me to pay off that card at £10 a day I may well have given up before I started. But I didn't (I don't think I even really knew what the balance was when I started). Had I considered that I would need to find extra money at the milestones then I would probably have said I couldn't afford it. But I didn't do it because I had to, I did it because I wanted to, and somehow I managed to afford it, and loved it - the best "spend" I'd ever made!

The positive mindset that paying MY NUMBER from MY CARD every day created, made amazing things happen which I had not anticipated and would have claimed I could not afford. I paid off my first card in record time.

I hear you. "That doesn't sound much like an avalanche of epic proportions to me". You're right, it's not. This was just the snowball being created, the real avalanche was yet to come, when I started on my second card.

What Happens When I've Paid Off My Card?

You may think this is a very obvious question - of course the answer is you start on the next card. Absolutely. But there are a couple of things to take into consideration here.

You now have one less card to consider - CONGRATULATIONS if you have got to this stage. So you need to pick your next card. Use exactly the same process as before - pick a card, any card - I went for the one with the lowest balance again (this adds to the momentum as it gets paid off quicker).

Again, nothing is compulsory here, your own mindset will make certain things happen, and DO NOT do anything which will put you under undue strain. However, remember you were paying a monthly amount (perhaps just the minimum, but it was an additional amount to your daily payment) off your first credit card throughout the process? This amount no longer needs paying. Why? Because you have paid off your first card - congratulations! So, instead of treating that as a bonus, why not use it to accelerate the payment of your next card?

So let me give you an example - in £'s if you don't mind, please substitute this for your own currency. If you started with four credit cards, and you paid the minimum amount off each of them every month, let's say the minimum's, and YOUR NUMBER are approximately:

Card 1:   £120

Card 2:   £150

Card 3:   £180

Card 4:   £270

YOUR NUMBER: £ 10

Now you have finished paying off Card 1 you are £120 better off per month - let's go on a spending spree - new shoes, new coat; then out for dinner, yum. Yep, exactly what I would have done before I started using this system. However the system starts changing your mindset, and suddenly you are no longer thinking like that.

There are two ways you can use this to accelerate your debt freeness:

1. You could pay what you were paying to your first card (£120 in the example above) directly into your second card on a monthly basis (i.e. increase the monthly amount you pay to the second card from £150 to £150 + £120 = £270). In this situation you would pay the £270 off the second card once each month, and continue to pay YOUR NUMBER (£10), that you originally set, on a daily basis.

2. You could continue to pay the same monthly amount (£150) from the second card, but increase YOUR NUMBER to include what you would have used for the monthly payment off your first card (£120); and pay

this increased amount off daily. In the example, if we assume an average of 30 days in the month, the £120 divided between those 30 days would be £4 per day. So YOUR NUMBER for the second card would increase from £10 to £14, to be paid daily.

I used option 2, and increased my daily payments. But, there was another added effect here caused by my change from a negative to a positive mindset towards my debts. Instead of paying £14 per day I rounded it up to £15 per day - it was a nicer number, and I was really into this debt paying by now. Believe it or not, I was having FUN!!! (Do I sound sad or what?)

So, for my second card I would continue to pay off the minimum of £150 (along with the minimums for card 3 and 4) but I would increase my daily payment to £15 per day.

So now, this second card, although it had a higher balance than the first, looks set to be paid off just as quickly. Added to this the fact that my mindset still encourage those bigger payments at each milestone, and an even bigger one when it was almost finished; and my second card was paid off in super record time. Yippee! Debt Free here we come.

When I came to the third card (using the example above) I should have increased my daily payment by £4.50 to £19.50 (£150 / 30 = £4.50). You guessed it, I rounded it up - but this time not to £20. I was on a roll, my mindset was driving me, I rounded it all the way up to £30! Did I manage? Sure I did. Did I suffer? No, I can honestly say I didn't. I may have struggled a bit more to boost the amount at milestones, but they were coming up so fast anyway it really didn't matter. Now I had an avalanche!

But remember, you only do this with an amount you are comfortable with. I was comfortable with my amount, although it was stretching me. Your positive mindset is what will drive you and help you to set a number which you will be amazed you can afford. That mindset may also try to push you a little too far at times, so remember that if the amount you are paying daily starts to put you under strain, you can always, and should, reduce it - DO NOT allow your mindset to turn negative again by putting you under stress.

So is this looking a little more like an avalanche to you? Well, it's not quite over, there is a little more snow to gather on our journey to being debt free.

One thing that often happens with a credit card company is that when they see you can pay off your debts they want to encourage you to spend more. Dangerous you say. Well, you can use this to your advantage.

One way in which they encourage you is to give you a 0% offer on a balance transfer - once I started clearing my cards I had numerous of these. Since we know our debts are now, after years of burying our heads in the sand, in control, why not take advantage of not having to pay some of the interest. When you get an offer like this it is worth taking. Move the maximum you can onto a 0% offer to reduce the accumulating interest, then leave that card until the end (or until the 0% offer is over). Even if you do not get around to paying the transfer off before the 0% offer has finished at least you will have had that period without any interest whilst you focused on other amounts which were accumulating interest - so it has to be a win for you.

So now, not only are you managing to pay off your debts whilst feeling good about them, but you are even managing to reduce the overall amount you have to pay.

Do we now have an avalanche?

What Not To Do

So I've told you what to do to become debt free:

Pay off YOUR NUMBER from YOUR CARD

Set a REMINDER to do the same again tomorrow

And I have explained how this can avalanche so you end up paying off all your debts much faster than you thought possible. All this is designed to change your mindset to your debts from negative to positive. Provided this mindset changes to positive then all of this avalanche will happen naturally. However, in order to ensure your mindset changes there are a few things you MUST NOT do.

So here is a list of the things you MUST NOT do:

- DO NOT set YOUR NUMBER so high that you struggle to make the payment each day, or have to change your lifestyle significantly to meet the payments. This is particularly important in the early stages of using the system. If you find yourself struggling then reduce the amount you pay daily.

- DO NOT spread YOUR NUMBER across multiple cards. You must pay YOUR NUMBER from ONE CARD each day. If you can afford more then pay it off the same ONE CARD. Your mindset will change from negative to positive much quicker if you see results quickly. Seeing one card paid off is a fantastic result and does wonders to your mindset. You know you will get round to the other cards, just pay off the minimum on a monthly basis, as usual, and don't worry about them until their time comes.

- **DO NOT** decide to multiply YOUR NUMBER by seven and then just pay it once a week. This whole system is based on changing your mindset towards your debts and making you focus positively on them. If you are only making a payment once a week this will not happen. The frequency of the payments is crucial to the success of the system.

- **DO NOT** stop paying the minimum amount (or some other predefined value) off any of your cards, including the one you are focussing your daily payments on. Your daily payments should be additional to any normal payments you would make.

- **DO NOT** worry. Period. Anything you are doing to reduce your debts is better than nothing. Do not worry whether you have picked the right card to start with - it doesn't matter, any card will do. Do not worry if you think YOUR NUMBER is too small or too large - you can always change this at any time. The real key is that you take the action. Taking the action regularly will cause a change in your mindset. Once you are in a positive mindset your mind will sort out all the details for you.

- **DO NOT** worry if you miss a payment (provided it is a one off due to not being able to get access to the bank, or not having enough money to pay with). DO NOT try to catch up with the payment by paying double the next day (unless you really want to and can manage to without undue strain). Just carry on as normal paying YOUR NUMBER from YOUR CARD each day. If you miss a day it will not make a huge difference. But if you start worrying about it you will change your mindset from positive to negative.

- DO NOT do anything that will cause you massive inconvenience when following the system - unless your positive mindset is driving you of course! If you apply the system so strictly you end up massively inconvenienced then you will retain a negative mindset and the system will not work. For example, it was inconvenient for me to pay MY NUMBER from MY CARD every day. I decided that I would pay EVERY WEEKDAY, this suited my lifestyle, and it worked beautifully (I did used to sneak an odd weekend payment in here and there when I was on a roll). Likewise, if you have to pay your payment in at the bank but cannot get there everyday then do it when it is convenient (having saved YOUR NUMBER up each day) - preferably try to make this at least once a week.

- DO NOT worry if you have to use your card to make a payment for something. Unfortunately life gets in the way of our plans sometimes, if you have to use your card then that's fine, just don't stop paying YOUR NUMBER from it each day.

If you can have a positive mindset towards your debts, so much so that you get excited about paying them off, instead of getting a big headache; and you can focus on them enough to make a difference, then you will succeed in being debt free. This system, if you follow the two simple steps every day:

Pay off YOUR NUMBER from YOUR CARD

Set a REMINDER to do the same again tomorrow

will give you that positive mindset and the focus you require to make a massive difference. All you need to do is follow the two steps and everything else will happen naturally.

What Happens in an Emergency?

Emergencies happen. Life gets in the way of all your best laid plans. What you have to remember is that paying off your credit cards does not cause an emergency to happen. On the other hand, paying off your credit cards can turn what would have been an emergency into just a real pain in the derrière.

Let me explain. When I started this system all of my credit cards were maxed out (and had been for years, even though they kept increasing the limits). All my bank overdraft limits were maxed out - I even applied for a big increase in one of these and was refused! I needed to do something. I seemed to be living off the tiny amounts that were left on the cards once I had paid the bill. It was ridiculous! I borrowed from Peter to pay off Paul and all the debts remained at the highest level they could be. Sound familiar?

Well, less than a year after I started using this system, and was feeling great, I got a BIG bill. Now I'm not talking about a £1,000, or even £5,000 bill. I'm talking about a £25,000 bill. WOW! Not pleasant. Did I know it was coming? Well, kind of, but I didn't expect it to be anything like THAT big. This WAS an emergency! If I had been in the same position I had been the year before I think I would have run away to Rio De Janeiro - if only I had enough credit left on my card for the ticket! But because I had done such amazing things in paying off my cards I actually managed to pay it - it was a struggle, but nothing like the struggle it would have been the previous year.

So the moral of the story is, if you manage to pay off at least some of your credit card debt, not only does it get rid of those terrible headaches, but it gives you a buffer for those real emergencies. And when you do need to use it for those real emergencies, because you have done it once before, you know you have the capabilities of paying it off again - without the pain!

For me, using this system has given me a very positive mindset, not just to paying off my credit cards, but to the whole value of money. I can still go out and have a good time. I can still spend it on stupid things occasionally, but I do tend to get much more value from it. I don't spend money just to drown my sorrows of owing so much money anymore. I really think twice about putting anything on a credit card, but I will still do it if I need to - but there's the difference, if I NEED to, and I feel great about that.

This system is not asking you to change your lifestyle or thinking. Follow the two small steps each day:

Pay off YOUR NUMBER from YOUR CARD

Set a REMINDER to do the same again tomorrow

and YOU will naturally change what needs to change for YOUR life and YOUR happiness. Two minutes a day, that's all it takes.

DO IT NOW!

Need more help, or willing to share your story?

If you are willing to share your story, or you will like some help or clarification on any aspect of this guide, then please feel free to contact me:

Facebook: http://www.facebook.com/HowToPayOffCreditCardDebt

Twitter: https://twitter.com/PayCardDebt

Google +: https://plus.google.com/u/0/b/105077633875831896003/105077633875831896003/posts

Website: http://suemaddock.com/howtopayoffcreditcarddebt/

www.ingramcontent.com/pod-product-compliance
Lightning Source LLC
Chambersburg PA
CBHW061521180526
45171CB00001B/285